OF MICS &

PENS &

GODS &

OTHER COLLEGE

COURSES

By Mariah C. Barber

All Rights Reserved

Contact: MariahCBarber@gmail.com

Cover design by Kayah Oluronbi

ISBN-13: 978-1542944083 (CreateSpace-Assigned)

ISBN-10: 1542944082

Dedication

This is for all those late nights in 94 and the people who touched my spirit between then & now. When we left handprints in paint on the four walls of that apartment, you all simultaneously left them on the walls of my heart forever.

Author's Note

Lying in my old bed in my childhood room, reflection has found me at this late hour and I am thinking about all that has transpired over the past couple days. I walked across a stage twice to a mispronunciation of my name to get a piece of paper rolled up that symbolized a diploma that I won't receive for three to five weeks and I smiled at camera flashes until my cheeks were weak. Not to sound cynical, but is this what I had waited for, is this what family came miles to see, is this what I had prayed for, and paid thousands of dollars to achieve? The answer was no! I was not proud of a weekend of glory or one single ceremonious occasion and that was normal. Instead I am proud of my accomplishments over four whole years. I am looking at how far I have come since birth. Remembering all my realizations about what I am passionate about, my awakenings to what and who makes me happy. All the late nights where I pushed my body to get the job done, all the tears about self-doubt and disappointment, all the tough stuff that has made me resilient and showed me I really can endure. I walked away from that moment on stage, a bit unimpressed because I didn't graduate in May. I have been graduating every time I overcame an obstacle or reached a new height in my life. All along I was turning my tassel as I turned each page of my journey and I didn't even recognize it. The only difference is …now the world can see the woman I have always been becoming. In this moment, all the excess marble has been chipped away to reveal a finished masterpiece, me. I am beautiful, you are beautiful; let's continue to graduate with each passing day…

Acknowledgements

To Mom and Pops thanks for always believing in me even when I doubted myself, you forbid me from giving up

To my brother, Nigel knowing that you're following in my footsteps keeps me walking a straight and narrow path

To my Aunt Lillie you will always be my first introduction to black poetry I am eternally grateful

To my editor Emani thanks for helping make sense of the jumbled art in my head

To my anyone I've ever loved unrequited or not you inspired a part of every poem

To my sister friends you give me the courage to write

To my brothers from another mother thanks for pushing my pen

To Word of Mouth thanks for always editing all my rough drafts WOMM

To my church home thanks for my first standing ovation

To my grandparents because of you I am

To Maya Angelou because of you I am

To God because of you I am

Table of Contents

Part I

Black Dolls, Beanie Babies & Barrettes

Genesis

I think I found poetry around the time,
My vocal chords decided to go on strike,
Refusing to hold up any more high notes.
Growing out of my desperation for talent- (because being the only
youth choir reject means you get a lot of shit)
& I know that sounds like a contradiction-
 but so is the war being waged between my spirit, mind and soul
Only to take a greater toll on this body
– That was paying through countless nocturnal nights
When rampant ideas knocked on my brain's door at the most
ungodly hours.
But despite my great grandmother's warning that nothing good could
happens after 3 am
More often than not, I found myself inviting all those thoughts in
I found myself surrendering to the invasion with white flags, in the
form of crumpled up pages
Scribbled on with my thoughts bordering insanity
- provoking poems in tandem with the sound of the seashell
If you hold it up to you ear and listen ever so softly
…every time I turn pages---
It's my own form of the parting of the red sea.
As lukewarm watered down words, unthaw my soul after what felt
like the coldest winter ever
I was baptized the first time my eyes made love to Maya Angelou and
was blessed enough to see Joshua Bennett's words walk on water
In that moment, hair dripping wet with homophones,
I realized that their religion and my religion sounded the same but
had two different meanings
Cause you see, I began to delve into poetry deep as prayer.
And since then I have been faithfully confessing all that I feel
between congregations of commas, and sitting in pews of pauses,
confessing to white pages my hopes to my dreams filling up books
Not only stowed away for Sunday's, because you can spit and write
anywhere with nothing to wear
But skirts of stanza,
Bold line button ups and
Your heart on your sleeves

Yes, I have a strong faith in poetry.
 I am so devout. I want to memorize verses I haven't even written
yet.
Rhyming commands me to love articulation and commune with
content.
And Lord knows I may not be convinced of theories of splitting
Adam's and Eve's, but I am an avid believer in metrical composition
Which is a fancy way of saying, in the constant cycle of sin,
I'll always translate my transgressions into tempos
About from daylight to deities-choosing to clap on and off beat
because there are not many rules here
Which is why I am content with my role here as the 13th disciple
The broke starving poet
Since there is not much tithing around the collection of emotions
that you can only decorate your soul with
I can imagine my ribcage looks like stanzas of sermons and behind
that is a heart murmuring with metaphors
 run through with sacrificial blood
repenting for all my constant repetition.
You see the doors of churches, temples and mosques close
But I will always have the immaculate cross
 that is created
When my pen combines with paper
To touch my innermost thoughts
In short, I am somewhat of a swearing saint-
Serving Poetry
I mean God
Most devoutly

Those Old Sayings

Mama always said
When it thunders, the devil is beating his wife
When it rains, it means
She cries
When its sunny he's bringing her flowers to apologize
I have always wondered where God is at during these times

Hunger Pains

I've never gone to bed hungry
When I had nothing
I ate my poetry for dinner

I remember the day like it was yesterday
I was twelve
Climbing trees taller than my wildest dreams
I was honeysuckle sweet
Lightning bug filled skies
Kissed boo boos mixed with bandages over scrapped knees
Evening bike rides & easy bake oven recipes
Two on two basketball games &
Allergic to the birds & bees
I had just figured out me
& then
That shit stopped everything
The menses
When womanhood came knocking on my door she called herself a
lot of things
But she didn't call before to let me know she was coming
Aunt flow
Cousin red
& the Crimson tide all came flowing in
No one other than my father was home
He said put a towel in your pants
Until mama gets home
& I learned right then & there how uncontainable
How Uncomfortable having the ability to give life is
...
What an anomaly to be a mammal that bleeds for a week & doesn't
die
To be the true apple of God's eye
I often wonder how remarkable a woman is shedding a part of
herself & still moving through life without missing a beat

Running for public office
Teaching your kids
Climbing Everest
Growing crops
Managing stocks
Learning to kick box

Studying & skydiving & breaking world records in the Olympics
All during her time of the month

So, complain again about how hard life is as a man
I know a magic force that only my women possess to push
Pick themselves up by their bootstraps
Even in heels and
& keep moving with a Tampax

If only those commercials showed the real things we did
We'd run the world period in vibrant
Colors most off the spectrum you can even see, much less fathom
Men obey traffic signals
But our routines don't stop for red lights
We are the decedents of our mothers
A force of nature it's only right
We control life

Self-Hate

I've always known one day there would be a movie written in my
name
And of course, I would have all creative rights to the story

So, I'd do all the casting directing & editing myself
And for this tantalizing tribute,
The entire thing would be Fantasia Barino style

Yes, everyone would play themselves
That way I wouldn't have to fear losing my brother's innocence in
some young junky Jaden Smith star lookalikes stunt double of a smile

And I wouldn't have to search the world for the effervescence of my
father's gold thumb
That way I'd be sure our hand holds were still lock and key tight

And I would film my grandmother's wisdom before it unraveled into
a peppered gray roll of film
Mirroring her hair
Shriveled up into the grain of salt the size she told me to take their
advice with

All this would be in front of the camera with 5 D features

So, you could taste my kind of womanhood
You could see all the silence
And then lick the pain from the screen

The lifetime reality of TV without reality TV
Yes, mine would be unscripted
Because my story will be right the first time
Like the things, you wish you listened to already applied
My feature film will have no regrets

Because you won't be there

That's right this script doesn't include my skin tone
It got written out in the re edits
Like America's history

Critics will call it a potato peeled to perfection
The second coming of Michael Jackson without the fructose coloring

But you see this is the only way I know this story will go according to plan

That my mother can give birth to me & witness my first cries without
replicating them because she knows what a black encasing has
awaiting for it in environments like these

And this film will be independent
Because it would have been safe to ride my two-seater bike alone in
my suburban white neighborhood
Without fear of "Do you live here?" stares
Or dip cans thrown out of half rolled down windows and mouths
hugging the word niggah between teeth

It would finally be more parts romantic comedy and not tragedy
with my first love being reciprocated
Because now I'll have a dirt-free complexion
so, that my Tom Boy is less recognizable
 so, that I look like I've climbed more trees
then hung from them

So, that I can be loved instead of overlooked
And in this version I won't have a dialogue of questions about why I
get straight As

& I am in the advanced placement classes of my high school because
I already look the part

I'll have more time so this shall be a short film because
I won't have to reteach my beauty
To myself
Like a course, I always skipped
I can just follow pop culture
I won't have to make up with the mirror because
I won't break it with my ugly hue in the first place

Speaking of places
Forget the Oscars
This piece will make people so penny proud
We will have to recreate the award so it better suits my reels of reality

And imagine how much action I will avoid with no need for a stunt
double
Like think of all the white people who won't be touching my hair
& I'll never have to start my natural transition
 cause let's be honest, that is a constant struggle
& with my lack of Ebonics, the English language will hit me as less of
a shock
& I won't be racially profiled or hurt myself &
I can shop without being followed around the store & I can actually
find clothes in my size big enough to fit my ass--pirations
Which would be attainable
& I mean I won't be able to twerk or dance in general
 but I mean some sacrifices will have to be made
 to be this close to white Jesus's genes

After all its ok if I give all my seasoning away in becoming a delicacy
This doesn't need much culture it's not a documentary

I've always known one day there would be a movie written in my
name
In big bright white lights

Nut I
can't
sell out
for fame
be estranged from who I am
I'm married to my melanin

Bark (Fallen Tree)

This is the story about a girl
No, a boy
Never mind it's really about the carved-out heart on the oak tree
 that bark could never mend from becoming broken
My childhood swing sat on the branches of trees
I don't think they were oak though
I can't remember I've repressed most of those memories
Except I could never forget that time my brother followed me up
into a tree and when I climbed down he couldn't get back to the
ground
That tree was cedar, I think
I wish I could say that was the last time he followed into my
footsteps and went off the path
Lost himself
Got stuck
Lost his footing on this earth
That tree must be full of rot by now like this love
Gods a funny guy
How he gives us a lifetime to come full circle
I bet we look like mice in a maze
I hope one day I can reach the cheese
by that I mean heaven not money
Even though a little extra cash for this broke college student
wouldn't be the worst thing in the world
I like to think he's in heaven
No matter what the pastor says
 I think God empathizes with slit wrists
more than he condemns them
After all he's such a funny guy
After all we're just mice in a maze to the man upstairs
He knows we are bound to make mistakes
Don't mistake my last line by skimming over it
That was a direct reference to the book of mice and men
It was my brothers favorite growing up
One of the few things
I remember before the blast
The gun in that book almost mirrored the one my brother used

As he leaned up against the old cedar tree
I wonder if there are trees in heaven
Another maze in the sky that resembles this one on earth
My brothers illuminated my dreams a lot lately
I haven't gotten a lot of sleep lately
I lied about the dreams
I've been lying wide eyed consciously thinking
I blame dreams a lot more than reality
It makes my truths
 easier to accept
I loathe trees
That's why I moved to this concrete jungle
To avoid reminders
To avoid thinking about childhood
To forget
To recreate my maze
To accept God is still a funny guy
That way I can't fucking hate him almost
more than my brother for leaving me
or myself for letting him
I hate trees
Cause they remind me of heaven
And arms
Like the one he carried to that tree
Or those arms I can no longer bury myself in
Or those cackling arms
Those branches
In those trees
Constantly taunting me
About the things, I can never touch again
The tallest tree I knew
Rioted from the inside and fell
And I wasn't around to hear it
Do you think my brother made a sound?

5"5'

From what the textbooks portray.
 Mahatma Gandhi stood at about 5'5
A rather frail looking man
 I'm sure could have only been 100 pounds, soaking wet
But the strength he carried in his heels
was enough to weigh out the shackles of apartheid
that had held India in imbalance for centuries
The peace that he exuded from his palms pressed together in prayer
was enough to change the crooked views
 buried deep in generations of hate
resetting even DNA straight
My brother stands at a solid six foot one
More head than body
I had no idea of the strength he bore in his bones
Only a junior at my old Alma Mater
His almond eyes have always possessed a sense of hidden wisdom
Knowledge well beyond his mere sixteen years
My mother called me at last week in the smallest voice
I've ever heard escape her lips
Her words hit me like a sucker punch to the ribs,
Her voice pin pricking all the air from my lungs
When she uttered the words:
Riah, what has gotten into your brother?
Who he is trying to be Gandhi or something?
Refusing to eat because I won't sign his paperwork to join the new
LGBT gay group at the high school.
What do you know about this?
It took me a moment to process the full of all she said
but after sometime I replied
 with as much reverence as you can hold for a queen
who's just lost the last droplet of respect as she denounced her
throne by clumsily dropping her last sentence
I'll talk to him
I've always wondered if the dial tone
that soon hit my mother's eardrum
was more like a red flag
or a cold shower

calling for her to wake up from her complacency
To open her eyes and ears to the world around her to see the beauty
in what she intended to be an insult

Because I'm proud to call my brother a freaking modern day Gandhi
in a world full of bigots
I wish she could clear the hate from her sight
cause like oil its left her blinded to what true love looks like

If my brother was Gandhi
I would be his bhindi
His third eye
guiding him through the destruction of this world
I would warn him that they will try to bend and break him
But that's why God built his bones like white columns on a temple
That's why God put all that knowledge between your temples
I would show him how they would try to break him
 bend him into society's tight fitting molds
Try to turtle neck his soul
But his heart was never meant to be covered or closed
Leave that to the doors and windows
So, when they will try to straitjacket his personality
Know in the mist of four white colored walls
You're far from crazy
That's just the world's way of trying to put you in another box
But always meant to be more of a circular man to me
Full of unity and life
You're in good company
All compasses and cloudscape lenses
Hell, people even tried to make this earth flat out of fear too
So, you see past prejudice and for that the world will always seem
threatened
You must be a Mahatma of a man
Taking their advice with a grain of salt
Because you remember in another life you too had to protest that too
And when you didn't join America
they tried to beat you into compliance
and water you down your truth
But know Gandhi was imprisoned too

and they never had even the slightest handle on his soul
So, stand even when others are too foolish to sit
Pray even when they say your cause is already forsaken
Call out even when the abyss is so dark you assume you fell on deaf
ears
Cause today more than ever this world needs a person as spherical as
you to lead it
Name it
And call it
And if you must sign truth when ignorant hands are either too shaky
or in clinched fists
Cause sometimes forgery is necessary when no authentic love
surrounds you
And I love you
Even when the whole world forsakes you
& After sometime
I realized I never actually hung up on my mother
just clicked over to the other line
Hell, When Gandhi is calling me
Who am I to keep him waiting?

My Apologies co-written with Munazza Abraham

Contrary to popular belief Madam CJ Walker did not invent the perm
Also know, as the white stuff or creamy crack
 the relaxer was designed by the child of former slaves
 in 1877 by Garrett M. Morgan
The relaxer was designed as a topical cream
used to improve our appearance making African American hair more
malleable
I am the original crack dealer,
I conduct business so smooth that I'm proud to say I've never been
incarcerated
Although I have handcuffed generations in insecurities
Misconceptions whispered into millions of young black girl's ears;
falsifying true beauty
I straightened the quirks that were your uniqueness
Burning away our history
And you thanked me, as you naively
Imprinted permanent waves of goodbye Mother Africa
I made you forget our home lands were never meant to run smooth
Back when bumps and humps exemplified beauty
& valleys were voluptuous,
But that time has passed now
I can hardly recognize our race with everything in this lines of
conformity
Corn rows were meant to remind us picking up cotton made us who
we are
The last time I remember lines like this, we were lying like cargo on
boats
I orchestrated the trade embargo, between white supremacy &
African American culture
And all the while I sacrificed our roots
I am apologetic, I provided the blade to slit
I am apologetic, I provided hells fires to lit
My forest once spoke volumes, crying each time a tree of mine fell
and no one was around to hear it
Hair isn't silent, cracking beneath the sizzles as if
Ancestral and chemical bonds were broken!

I apologize
I severed my mind from my scalp
Too late to regain consciousness when the last follicle has dropped
teenaged receding hairlines,
As if retreating scared, too young to fight on the front lines
This was one battle perhaps we were not ready to fight, we charged
in head first,
Giving the enemy just what they wanted,
head first, body next, soul last
As history depicts
We are still slaves to the page, never once opting to pick up the pen!
With excuses of her naps are too thick,
I don't know what to do with that!
As if it's easier to become a dark alchemist in your kitchen,
than to ask a question, pick up a braid magazine or fuckin YouTube
it!
You let him pull the strings,
We're his favorite puppet, cut by the same cotton cloth, tragedy
We try to fix the mistake God never made, blasphemy.
We're his black-faced raggedy Anne
Let him pull thin the strands, unravel the coils stitched in our skin,
never safe from societal tools, caused a few screws loose,
no wonder we're mad black women…
And we are the catalyst to our own destruction
But we don't care, logic can scream and shout as long as we can flip
our hair.
Because for better or worse, even a slave will come to see
You will never be allowed to be who you want to be.
But you will try.
Over and over again,
you will try to personalize this hell
To be pretty
And this purgatory
Is the only near-natural cycle, pattern, curl, coil, or ring, you will ever
call your own.
And I am sorry.
I am apologetic I am the beginning with no ending,
Your natural addiction
To unnatural beauty.

Dear You

Dear no one
You are going to be somebody someday
One day sooner than you think
Don't neglect to cherish the skinned knee memories
Look at them as reminders of cool breeze bike rides
You will need this joy for future days
when life will ride you harder than your two seater
And the emptiness will remind you of your benevolent skinned heart
Dear no one
The stork is a lie
Babies do not come from lying in bed with the opposite sex
I don't care what the movies say
I pinky promise
Although you will learn in later days that holds little weight
Dear no one
You won't grow out of the asthma messy allergies to grass
Dear no one
You are going to be someone one day
Never mind the bullies that call you four eyes
They just notice the two in your head one in your mind and your
third eye
Hug your grandmother more for days
 when you will reach out for her and find no embrace
Dear no one
I read the poems you scribble in your crack head handwriting on
desks and no matter what they say
 I think it's a beautiful juxtaposition between obscurity and insanity
Practice your handwriting less
No one could read newton's notes either
But that didn't stop him from mapping out the mathematics behind
the gravitational pull pushing down his lead to page
Dear no one
I know you dream of becoming the first female African American
president
And even if someone beat you to the punch
I think your poetry could be the vehicle to perform for her one day
Keep dreaming

You aren't too far off
Dear no one
I know you only punch your brother
Because it's poetry
Symbolic of what white America will do to a black man
Dear no one
I know growing up in the suburbs sheltered you
Stop apologizing for their uncomfortable
Walk tall
Cherish not having to always look up to them
You had your growth spurt early so being the tallest in your class
won't last long
Dear no one
Tell someone about the touching
Anyone
Just someone
Dear no one
Accepting God into your heart is still one of the best decisions you
ever made
Don't ever doubt your faith
Or yourself
Remember the holy in you when you notice the holes
Dear no one
Throw out the ADD medication
I like you the way you are
Even the loud, forgetful
Late & accident prone parts
Nothing worthwhile ever came without being waited on
Dear no one
You don't marry Bow Wow
Or dribble your way into your dreams
You've always been more
Like Maya
Then like Mike
Dear no one
Everyone makes the youth choir
You cannot sing
I repeat cannot sing
Leave it to the other Mariah that touched the world before you

Quit
I repeat quit
Focus your efforts on spoken words that stir the soul like a song
Dear no one
It is all worth it
The ass whoopings
Ice cream truck sticky fingers & blue lips
Growing pains
And unending chore lists
Dear no one
All your dreams will come true in the most
Unconventional ways possible
And enjoy the surprises
Because life is a gift
And the universe is just a party God shocked us with
Dear no one
I know you will never get this
Because I don't want to send it &
Risk messing up this continuum
We refer to as time
We all know time machines bring trouble
So, I plan to burn this
With as much fire as your passion

Reflections

Lately love sees
Lust in the mirror
And as a result, these days
People cannot tell the two apart
Or recognize
The difference

Wall Art

Make a living museum of yourself
Charge them all
To pay attention

Part II

Amor y Dolor Live on the Same Street

Alcoholics Anonymous (A.A.)

Tips on Dating the drunkard's daughter

When I tell this story backwards it hits the throat with a little less
sting
Less like a shot
More deluded
This story goes down like a mix drink trying it's best to hold on to
the sobriety of water

When I Ieft her & told, her it was over, it was over
It was the first straight line I had walked in three months

You should know when you date the town drunks' daughter what the
town will never tell you

Her hair & skin & hands will be as wild black soft & bitter as freshly
crushed grapes between toes from Martha's Vineyard

Her lips will taste of birthday cake vodka, begging you to be drunk
any merry in their embrace

And she, she will leave your sheets smelling of shot glass spilling over
with shame yet trying their best to hold on to the memories of the
nights prior

Her body will be made of coke glass figure but full of toxins
Glass embedded in her heels from all the egg shells she's been forced
to walk on for all these years
She pretends they're glass slippers and is waiting for Prince Charming
or the next best thing brave enough to rescue her
from the tower, she's built in her spine
The only thing keeping her standing upright through this sorrow

You see, all her life she's been drowning in the moat that surrounds
her

From placenta to the liquids constantly filling her father's throat
Your name is one of the few things she has learned to stomach

Know that, when you leave you will be inherently perpetuating the
belief she has that nothing ever can hold on to her like daddy does
his drinks, not even daddy

Cold showers & coffee can't sober her
You see, the drunk's daughter doesn't know she has a problem

& You, you have become her latest vice

Drunks don't teach restraint very well so all she knows is excess of
emotions, excess of emotions, excess of emotions

She wasn't a believer in love until she met you

She figures if you can hold a bloody fistful of her brokenness in one
hand and still, find the strength to crack a smile
There must be a God

She drinks to cry & cries at the fact she drinks
Red Wine bottle mouth smiles open wide so you can see her teeth
She lets you inside
The first time she says she says I love you
It sounds like shattered Hennessy glass bottles and piano key
symphonies

She has begun to gulp you down before even knowing you're in her
grasp

& she, she's going to try to hold you like a counter covered in empty
beer bottles
Give you support, uplifting nothingness in place until it can be
disposed of or recycled
In the next relationship
But you know nothing of this yet

Now you think

She's going to quench your cotton mouth thirst
with all the words left unsaid in your last relationship

Eventfully you will flip open her inhibitions like a can's tab

& pray you won't fizzle

The drunk's daughter will be hesitant to believe your promises; she's
used to waiting until last call only to encounter disappointment

But you will prove yourself because this, this is one of the greatest
pursuits you have gone through and it's anything but trivial

Getting to know her is like a drinking game; you take turns, shot after
shot
You play Never Have You Ever in order to find out what she likes

There is an unsolved mystery behind her eyes you are attracted to
You have no idea what you are getting into but then again that's the
draw
So, you pluck another card
Trying to breathe life into this circle of death
The first times you kiss something's not right but you figure it's like
unscrewing a bottle and eventually you will get it off

We hit it off
Ran into each other like old friends in a bar and struck up a
conversation like a match

Two flaming shots, we took each other back
Figured we might be each other's reborn Phoenixes or maybe a fire
to keep warm by while healing up for the next

When she approached me with the initial hello I was so taken aback
As if there had to be whiskey on her
Breath of lies
Starting over with her was such a new sobering beginning
 or so it seemed sharing laughs over first drinks

We meet & greet
& I hoped to never say goodbye
& I still don't know if this is a poem about the last woman I loved
Or how alcohol has become my latest mistress

Taste

I brushed my teeth
For five hours, this morning
And I still taste your name

Fuck Butterflies

Forget the butterflies
In my stomach, I feel pterodactyl wings
Flapping harder every time your thighs rub together
Right to left
Your hair and hips swing on the playground where our eyes play freeze tag
And you're it but I want you to catch me
I want you to bury me in your love
And lavish in your beauty all day
The way I imagine your honey brown skin would soak in the sun on a beach
Boy, do I need a vacation!
Because my mind has been hard at work racing like a full-time job
I hope you're happy with my work
& will consider me for a promotion because with me as the CEO
I just know we can make millions
Still all the money in the world, won't hold a candle
 to that million dollar smile
God somehow entrusted you to possess
Maybe its payment for when he clipped your wings and placed your feet on solid ground
In this world, you are my world
So why don't you walk my way
The way you do in my dreams where Frank Ocean reads my mind and sings out your soundtrack
played on my heart strings as you pull on them
Like the harp, you must have used to play in the clouds
I empathize with how the dinosaurs felt when their era was ending
because when your hand brushes up against mine, comets hit the earth
Although that extinction thing must have been bullshit
Because I know at least one dinosaur that still lives inside me
And comes back to life each time I breathe you in
So, when you ask me if you give me butterflies I say no
Butterflies don't do you justice
You give feelings back to the fossils
I thought died in me long ago

.... Nicotine

About last night........
being with you was
like kissing an ashtray
on the forehead, every
morning before
breakfast

it was the messy
& disgusting & perplexing
& so far from my routine
& so, beautiful
& risky
& jaw dropping
& maybe detrimental
but only in the most loving way

deep down I always knew
you were never supposed to make it
onto
my to do list

but sometimes
somehow when the sun
finds my eyes open
and confronts them
for cheating with the moon
again
it finds you shipwrecked
in the rubble around my irises
lost among
the passion & sweat & smiles & bites & bed

since the first night

I have seen your cigarette
bud fingerprints
leaving their marks
on my asthmatic heart

I know if I let this
It could easily
Kill me

but

you can make me

feel sexier than
breathing
can

Twelve Dollar Words

Petrichor
Is a noun
Meaning an earthly scent
Occurring when
Rain falls on dry soil
I learned this word
Exactly two days ago
My iPhone keyboard
Doesn't even recognize it yet
But I have been breathing in the aroma
Falling in love with the first rain droplets
To touch down
In a thunderstorm
After the warm since I was five
Isn't it funny?
How little we actually know
How there could be a twelve-dollar word
Floating around somewhere
Describing your favorite thing
And you would never even hear it
They say on average
 in our native languages
Our vocabularies
Consist of roughly 45 hundred words
The English language
My native tongue is
Made up of over a million
So, save your breath
When you try to tell, me you don't
Know what to say
…or how to covey to me
You want this
Don't
There are unspoken alphabets articulated in the silence
Ways with words your mouth
Could never even fathom
I understand, you simply don't

Have the vocabulary to describe me yet
And maybe you never will
Not even in three languages

Combinations

A list of a couple things I've noticed
1
If you watch the show The Fosters on ABC Family like I do & still
vote or are planning on voting as republican in the next election
Or
Watch Orange is The New Black and still think you can judge a book
by its cover
Or
Have ever agreed with anything out of Donald Trump mouth and
consider yourself a feminist
Fuck you
I hate you, you hypocrite
2
I make it a general rule to loathe hypocrites, the only exception to the
rule is if you are still in the closet; I can empathize with that
I understand being forced by family to pretend to be something
you're not
Just awaiting the day when your life can be reclaimed as your own
3
Speaking of closets.
The other when I was cleaning out mine; I found my caterpillars old
cage
Well it was more like a small plastic container with holes poked in the
top (yes, I had a pet caterpillar at one point, Okay? I was a different
kind of child).
I digress
Any way I found him outside and captured him; named him Benny
and fed him leaves
That winter he built a cocoon in the corner of the container
And I was so excited
After seven months, my family finally made me scrap the remains of
Benny from the container
They said if he was going to go through metamorphosis I
t would have happened by then
I later read online that water is very important to metamorphosis and
had an epiphany

I should have sprayed Benny bi weekly
I never cried for Benny
Or felt guilty
4
I can count on one hand with one finger the amount of times I've
cried this past year
When it happened, it wasn't at a funeral?
Or a hospital waiting room
Or a church
It was during the most heartfelt thing my ears have ever been blessed
enough to hear during a slam
And that's enough proof for me that when God speaks
It sounds like poetry
Fewer things are as reverent to me
5
I promised myself I won't rewrite this piece,
I can't change any of the lines
because they're already in the chronological order
They were meant to be
in
like my life seeming jumbled but laced with jewels
6
This began as a list of the things I hate and ended up being an
autobiography
What does this say about me
Or how I love myself
7
I loved myself in parts and I began with the ones the mirror could see
first
Until I realized in the end of days we will all be turned inside out
And I've been undoing the damage ever since
8
I usually leave broken things alone
And try to fix things that are perfectly fine
The reason why you no longer take my calls
This is a testament to my love life
9
In this poem, I fixed all the things I said I wouldn't touch
Hit backspace and undo backspace then undo again

I'm still trying to stop my hypocritical tendencies
Say the things I mean and mean the things I say
But I'm a poet who turns herself inside out on stage for all to see
But is still too scared to tell her family about her and the one before her
I just watch OITNB & The Fosters on DVR enough for them to notice
It's just you were only beginning to love me for me when I uncovered something else
Until my confidence became another whole thing I needed to break
I think that's why I never cried for Benny
Only in the sanctuary of that slam
Because God's voice reminded me of love which reminded me
Of the pronouns, I would have to forge in my autobiography
I didn't want to face the truth
that I too may never leave this cocoon
Complete my metamorphosis
I may just keep repeating this never-ending cycle that is my life
952718346
987654321
672345189
123456789

10
Until I remember the original combination
And where the poem
I mean God's voice
Began

Nomad (Chicago)

I liked you
That is
Until
I realized
I was destined to
Fall in love with cities
& fall out of love with people
Home
Is where the heart is
But with me
With this heart made of sticks
When this windy city blows it all down
To twigs & nothingness
I will not
Quiver
I am well-traveled
In rebuilding
In living
In places, as
Unviable
As my chest

Which of the following is Right?
(Test Question)

Sometimes I get discouraged
That since my father
None
Of the men
I have encountered
Have had smiles
More Sunflower
Than seeds
I can't raise
You
Like my hand
In class when I have a question
Sometimes you get prompted by a question on God's test given to us
This life
Which of the following answers is correct?
& sometimes
There is
Nothing
To do
But leave it blank

―――

Deficiency

A year ago, today I saved you in my phone as Vitamin D
You were my sunshine
I thought I couldn't live without you
Fast forward to now
Most days it's dark but I'm breathing

Her

I used her luggage
Talk about baggage I claim
sand can leave the beach

Part III

Why Bad Things Happen to Good Black People

God, Our Father

I wonder

what kind of monster

lives under Gods bed

I bet it's an

abomination of a beast

a body attached to 12 heads

all resembling Judas

each with no face

solely a goulash mouth

 & filled with three serpent tongues

with skin that looks like

boiled

 up banishments

from the garden of Eden

coated in

unanswered prayers &

it feels

like blasphemy

bet it kisses

his sleep

like a sin, you

can't wash off

he calls

the worst nightmares

.... Mary

cause these memories

have to be

immaculate conception

Right?

God doesn't remember

his own thoughts fucking

Themselves into existence

he just closes his eyes

 & there, there

Miraculous no?

most believers don't know

Cause he's a private person

but God,

he's been battling

depression

for melanomas

if you pay attention

you can look up

his patient history

in the good book

you see right there

when he got bad

one episode he tried

to drown out

His own voice &

He almost did it too

 half dead half silent

For 40 days

He called the ark on himself

it arrived & saved him

Have you ever tried to save you from you?

Tried To end you by you

Sink & swim at the same time

It's impossibly possible

That time

.... he lost

I mean won

I guess it depends on how you look at it

Now God

goes to

his shrink at least bi weekly

& rainbow she makes sure everything is worked through

Even After the darkest & rainiest nights

I wonder if her office is near the one my father goes to therapy at

He won't tell

Me

He's private that way kind of like God

& I can't tell you

when & where he speaks

but all know Is our family is afloat

Again

So

He has to be talking to someone, right?

& Maybe he's talking to God

In some sort of twisted group therapy, I hope they can help each other find peace one day

I wonder what they talk about

Maybe the triggers or about how the depression

first started

My dad tells him when he lost his job

It was just something about not having anything to do with his hands all day

God says he had the same problem too

Said

All he wanted was to provide for his children

but they say they don't

need him

No more

They stopped putting hands together to pray

God & my father both know what it's like to hold the world in your palms and still feel empty

It makes you want to crush between your own fingers just to

Feel

something

 Anything

...

But the nothing

... But the numb

Sometimes I resent   God for allowing me to be swallowed whole by this disease

This monster carrying my bed on its back

How he watched me suffer

In silence

 drowning in my own distain

Now I know why maybe

he needed a meeting with a rainbow too

Busy to make a rainbow

My father

My God

I see the slit wrist red in the scriptures

I know there's some nights the angels hide all the razors & sharp nights

I know sometimes heaven can appear to be hell in your head

My God

I know the real reason you made

Joseph a carpenter

 just wanted someone skilled enough to build

 to coffin a Christ

The next time you felt dark enough to drown again

So, you didn't have to take the world with you

After you pinkie promised

Never to take US down again

My father says in the darkest depths of his depression he found God & I wonder who the lord found

A drift

How stirring

To be drowning in the same element walked on top of

My Father, My God

Do you bleed like the crucifixion?

Every time the sadness crosses your eyes

I know

He just needs someone to notice

The nothing he's feeling

The numb

We have to make him feel

To grab out for his hands

This debilitating disease takes pride in robbing you blind

No one can see all its taking from you until your gone

What do my father & I do when even God turns a blind eye?

Where do we find refugee from?

The constant flood in the silence what is counselling

Cause there's no way to talk your way out of a fight with a twelve-mouthed beast

Waiting by your bedside for a bad day ......

A friend of mine that studies physiology says patients dealing with depression, have a more realistic view of the world

And I wonder if God has that view because he's suffering it he built it

I pause I'm overthinking

And try to remember where this all

Started

Maybe in Genesis I can find the source

And stop it

It reads in the beginning was the word & the word was God & There is God in me

So, is this hereditary?

Should I be talking to someone too?

My father and my God

are both black men whose mental house is taboo

Mamas Always Said

I had no problem learning to
Look both ways before crossing the street
My issue has always been
Trying not to
Look back for too long

Blood Letting

Red blood, turned dry
now brown, brown boy blood
Cause when we die, we die darker

Afros

Our hair defies law
Gravity can't keep it down
Jim Crow can't either

Pavement Cracks

When I was seven years old
I would avoid sidewalk cracks like the plague
So as to keep my mother's back intact you see
And on the off chance my Converse happened to mingle even
slightly with the inside of the break between concrete
I would pray until my hands turned blue from the grip and my eyes
watered from how tightly I closed them
And I was sure God had gotten the message to spare my dear mother

A few years later and at 20
I hardly pray
I traipse across sidewalks without a thought of my mother

And ironic enough I can see her breaking
It started with the chemo
The poison the hospital appointments injected into her bi weekly to
keep her body from poisoning itself first
And I can't help but wonder if this started with the sidewalk as I
walked across it in my 6 inch stilettos last weekend
Club dress and alcohol ridden body
Reeking of gin and bad intentions
You see my mother has always been a saint
Which leads me to believe she can only be paying for my sins
And so, I watch her break
Next to frail were her hands
As her fingers retreat into her palms
As if to say a twisted goodbye to her own body
She struggles to do remedial tasks now
Like type
Or write
Or clasp her hands in prayer
The doctors diagnosed it rheumatoid arthritis
But I recognize it for what it really was
Revenge
This is God smiting me for all the years I spent with idle hands
On street corners

Letting the devil call them his own
On nights when I sold instead of getting a real job
When I pushed instead of pushing papers
And now my mother has no choice but to deal with the hand I dealt her
Last to go were her eyes
And as her brows furrowed and her vision faltered
I remembered how many years I wasted looking down at this earth instead of up towards the heavens
And how much time I spent fulfilling earthly desires
Instead of praising him
And as I watch my sins
Fold my mother's body into itself I can't help but wonder
How many of us are breaking down our own mothers like folding chairs?
instead of sitting with what we did
The less time we spend praying
Or doing right
Or leaving them up to worry at night
And I wonder how long it will take me to stop mistaking fault lines in the pavement for shortcuts
And walk the straight & narrow path
And I wonder how much more of her I have left
How much more pressure her back can bear
Before it breaks under the weight of my sins

Nooses Turned Capes

It's a bird
No, it's a plane
No, it's a black man & he's not falling & he's not hanging
He can fly
He's closer to heaven & not because he died
This time he's the good guy
What if in some alternate universe,
Black men were superheroes
All comic book characters
& heroic poses
Whirl winds of tights brawn & brains & saviors of damsels in distress
when they're not working their Clark Kent day jobs at a desk
If black men were super heroes
Every bang boom pow
would not be followed by another brother getting gunned down
 on the ground & a one sided story by the police
But merely bold comic book sans letters
 on colorful pages in action fighting scenes
& if black men were superheroes, would they work in collaboration
with the police
But behind closed doors so the public couldn't see
And my black male superheroes would be less violent & more
vigilante & my men of steel could bend bars
decreasing the egregious numbers of men of color behind bars
 & most of all if black men were superheroes,
They would be bulletproof
They would be immortal
They would be guaranteed a tomorrow
I mean sure there'd be kryptonite but if my black men were super
heroes
They wouldn't have to be Crips tonight
They would be less disposable & maybe then we could get some
positive representation in the media
And if black men were super heroes, they could develop gills to
breathe and never die on camera at the scene & Eric Garner would
still be alive

If my black men were ever allowed to be superheroes,
 they could tell stereotypes it's clobbering time
Black male superheroes could speak every language
so, Diablo never dies
If my black men were superheroes,
Could they fall in & live to get married to their one true love &
unwrite Shawn Bell's story
& if my black men were super heroes they
Could live to raise their sons & to see their son's sons raise more
black superheroes
Unlike Alton Sterling
If black men were superheroes, would Wolverine use his razor-sharp
blades to pick out his Afro
Would people marvel at their melanin?
Would black superheroes still shapeshift into a more docile creature
to be easier on their white washed eyes
If black men were superheroes,
Would we be fast as Flash and always be at the right place at the right
time?
If black men were superheroes,
Could they control the mind like Professor X?
Malcom that is
Would they use telekinesis to mobilize the people?
If black men were superheroes,
you'd let your white sons dress up like them before they go to sleep
Could we finally live long enough to grasp a dream?
If black men were super heroes & could travel through time
Could they go back and save thousands of black lives
Or would nothing change
If black men were superheroes, would you finally say their names
Would the Batmobile get pulled over more times?
Would you tell black superheroes to pull up their tights?
Would they still be good enough for Mary Jane?
If black men were superheroes and you could send up a signal so you
knew they were coming,
Would you still cross over to the other side of the street when you
see the hooded man swoop in on his feet
If black men were superheroes,
would there be a hashtag created called superhero lives matter?

Then another hashtag created to combat that
to say all civilian lives, matter too
I mean sure the superheroes are the ones out here risking their lives
but it's all for good measure right
If black men were superheroes and it made the news,
Would you even believe the byline?
Because they weren't painted as the victim or the villain this time

For Michael

When you impregnated Ms. Jackson
I'm sure the strings must have already been attached
This type of thing could have only been premeditated
Your plan to puppet, our dear boy
Manufacturing him to make you millions
You exploited your last name, so beautifully
An ingenious plan to create a product
Extrapolated of its ego
Full of dreams you injected with bleach
The color of the white blankets of wool you pulled over his eyes
Whispering things in his ear you knew were unattainable
The closest thing to truth you ever told him was the mantra
"Dance Michael dance, sing Michael sing"
You committed the only legal form to date of, child manslaughter
And the world sat back and not only watched,
But applauded,
But with every clap you convulsed
Body pretending it was you on stage bowing
You sold your son's soul,
For fame, fortune, and scented rose petals thrown at your feet
Still I must admire your drive
Your dedication
Creating a breed
To feed the hunger of your own dreams
You're not all self-serving
After all, as you toss and turn from your guilt,
At night when you can't find sleep,
Your son,
He rests in peace

Our Mouths

We're all bits and pieces of half told stories and hyperboles
About girls who swallowed their dreams whole and now they can't
stop spitting up fire
We call her ghetto,
We call her loud,
We call her black
But there's no silent way to birth a phoenix backwards
To teach a body to love after an abortion
To reteach a body that it is no longer a burning building awaiting its
impending doom
We're all bits and pieces of half told stories and hyperboles
About boys who transformed their bodies from home to a closet
So, understand every time he locks hands, winks or smiles at him; it's
a little more light getting under the door
Our words are all keys and locks with the power to close and open
doors
We must stop being so careless with our languages
Using our appendages so loosely
We must screw in our tongues
No more leaving mouths ajar
Be mindful of the mouths you have closed
Pay close attention to capitalization
How our first last and middle names
Start & end the same as God's
A constant reminder of how from the beginning we are all mirrored
in his image
So, every time your mouth forms around the word bitch
 it's just you coughing up the glass shards of your own muddled
reflections of your own mother Mary
How dare you use your God's so loosely?
Baptize our babbling
We're all half told stories and hyperboles

We choose words less wisely than we should
In a society with illuminated signs for vacancy, liquor, and tattoo
displaced off highways in all caps
And no signs of help
But who's writing our next chapters
Stop letting urban dictionary teach our children the origin & power
of their words
We're all half told stories and hyperboles
We must stop demeaning ourselves
In our meaningless lives
Learn our origins
My name is Mariah
It means God is my teacher
My father taught me the power of the language
He taught me we are all created in his images
We are all reflections of light
Bouncing off the roofs of one another's mouths
We are
The liquor, vacancy, and tattoo signs in all caps
We are bitch on all fours twerking to the beat that drops
We are all faggots who damn to each other to hell
We are all living in and for our mistakes
We are all our dreams
We are all abortion clinic lobbies
We are all lobbyist fighting for pro life
Aspirations and fears
We are all reflections
We are all niggers
We are all spicks
We're all pieces of half told stories and hyperboles
We are all what we speak in & out of existence
We are all half-told stories and hyperboles
until we find the truths
Train your language

Grandfather

He is a dead tree
All rot and bark, uprooted
Rings made of wrinkles

Harambe

if black men
were moved to the
endangered species list
I bet we'd have a bigger
turn out at the protest

Graffiti

Basquiat painting
crown the ghetto never kept
spray paint royalty

Part IV

Bookends for Never Ending Stories on Bookshelves

The View of A Sell-out

Raven-Symoné played a psychic
Plot twist
she can't understand her past

Heritage

Arching history
From my eyebrows and backbone
Still feels unnatural

Travel

Lost track of plane rides
When you're rich
You don't need the window seat

Burr

Others bundle up
Not me I've always felt the
Cold on the inside

10

Found John 3:16
In the back of my closet
Dust on my church dress

Smoking

Marlboro kisses
Only love ring finger knows
Temporary fix

Daddy Issues

Fictional father
Shadows in family pics
All you were was sperm

Pin Number

Debit card pin number
Her address in the projects
Reminds me to give

Shelter

His beard was a web
Ironic spiders call home
A man who is homeless

Eyes

Windows to the soul
If the left eye is lazy
Are half the blinds shut?

Life

Stop waiting for roses
You have been through enough shit
To be a garden

P

Boy, you fixed my favorite watch
And I still
Can't get our timing right

Rebel

She filled her body
Thirty-seven piercings and still
A hole in her soul

Sinner

Lipstick, tight dress
Drinking the weight of my sins
As you can guess, drunk

Mess

we loved like kids
with chocolate covered hands
in a black grandmothers'
all white room
it was messy &
we were never supposed to end up here
but how else can
love grace us
 with her presence
without a
little
unexpected chaos

Sticks & Stones

Poets admire bones
How they hold someone so broken
Or try

Eviction Notice

Pay no mind to those
Who try to break into your skin?
No home in their own

C Cup

Victoria Secret
make everything motherly
sexy for them

Part V

You Probably Thought Everyone Went Home from the Protest, The Dead Body is Still Here

Mike Brown co-written with Tony Dyer (Real Thought)

Autopsy 3,000,000,699
So, what do we have today?
Another black body pulled from white chalk outlines
So, that even in death we are confined
He had two shots to his ribs caged by marshal law
His lungs inhaled white supremacy
Then exhaled genocide
It could have killed him quicker than carbon monoxide
But in the cop's eyes he was already guilty
 Or maybe too impatient
He couldn't wait for another disease or murder
In that moment, he became the judge juror
Hell, even an executioner would have taken more time to decide
So, don't ask us why he did it because we will only report the truth
No more of the Fox news facade
No matter the size of your house or the car in your garage
There's a war going on outside don't tell me you can't hear the barrage
Like the cops say he reached for something
But the last time I checked it
The sky wasn't in his pockets direction
Arms reaching for his last words to God
Shot down, like an unanswered prayer
Left there like another character in their assassination
Now as they put his legacy on trail
They claim he was a born sinner didn't ever wait for the diagnostic to claim he died agnostic
It's such a cold world and all we really want to do is be free if only that's what it costed
When will all this racism be finished?
 He was the victim not the defendant, I'm fucking sick of it
…...Chill! As you know they have a lot more of them coming
True, so our youth are forced to fear the costumes they wear
Hoodies, rellos, music, even too long of a stare could lead to your last step

So, what is our world coming to what tragedy will be next?
Force to train our sons and daughters to have a fear of eye contact
Wouldn't want them to think your wallet was a gun or your phone was a knife
But even if you don't draw on them there will be a rest in peace mural painted every night
But we can't learn from Emmett unTill we unite
For heaven sakes, it was a whistle it wasn't rape
They're the ones taking things without asking
Stealing lives and futures
Lying to justify why they shoot ya
Truth is we're still living the same way almost two hundred years after plantation days \
Look closer at his cerebellum, we're still all mental slaves
Brainwashed as they whitewash our history then hang us out to dry
Like they did when they would lynch us and hang us by our feet
Except now they leave us dead for five hours in the street
Damn, he could have gone to college one day
Wait he was going to college on Monday!
How many days, weeks, years have their already stolen?
It's timeless like the perception of us at the bottom of the totem
Polls say over half of us hold racist belief
Since Obama got in office that number has increased
So, you mean to tell me we had the White House and people were still being taken from black homes!
Cause of death
Gunshot wounds
Four to the body, two to the head, one noose to the neck
Cause of Death
White Supremacy
A sickness engrained in minds
Passed like bread around dinner time it's created a myth of superiority
A tall tale they use to make us forget
They learned civilization from Africa, then brought us here and call us ignorant!
Cause of Death
We create class systems like Willie taught us
Separating ourselves

Until the brain becomes a cage and the body is a cell
Now we move in circles like vultures
Light skinned vs dark skinned
boujee vs ratchet
Good hair vs bad hair
The fact is we're all the same
All our roots are intertwined
So why does she have to be a bitch
Or him a spic
Or a nigger I figured
 We're all victims to the propaganda they perpetuate
We all can't be Malcolm or King but we all can participate
Find your gift give it to the people before your presence is gone
Stand together
Until then
Cause of Death
us

this is my gift to the people. I hope they receive it with open hands, minds, eyes & hearts.

Made in the USA
Lexington, KY
27 March 2017